"HE SENT HIS WORD AND HEALED THEM..."

—— PSALM 107:20

30 DAYS

of

HEALING

Connect to
God's Healing Power
With 30 Devotions and Prayers

PAUL RICHARDS

PAUL RICHARDS MINISTRIES

30 Days of Healing

Connect to God's Healing Power With 30 Devotions and Prayers
by Paul Richards

Copyright © 2014 Paul Richards
All rights reserved. PaulRichardsMinistries.org

First Print Edition © June 2014
ISBN 978-0-692-02651-9

All Scripture from the New King James Version 1982 except as otherwise noted.

New International Version: "Scripture taken from Holy Bible, New International Version (Registered Trademark) Copyright 1973,1978, 1984 by International Bible Society. Used by permission of Zondervan Publishing House. All rights reserved."

Cover photo by Silken Photography
Cover Design by Suzanne Fyhrie Parrott
Formatted for Publication by First Steps Publishing Services

Published by Paul Richard Ministries

For those challenged by illness, expressing
faith for healing is more than an act of belief,
it is an act of courage.

This book is dedicated to those who demonstrate
that courage, whether they realize it or not.

May God's healing power be yours.

Contents

Foreword

If you are reading this, you are probably in need of healing. If so, then you may also be dealing with associated challenges that can accompany the pursuit of wholeness, such as pain, fatigue, fear, and depression. It can be a lonely, even desperate, place. I know. I have been there.

If you ask Him, God will help. Not as a distant deity indifferent to your need, but as a Savior, a loving and protective Father, a committed healer whose heart yearns for your well-being.

This may be difficult to believe. If you are unsure of God's desire to heal you, to personally touch your life, you are not alone. Many struggle intellectually and emotionally with the idea of a "hands-on" God. I was one of those people. It took a miraculous encounter with Him to change my understanding.

I first connected to God's healing power in 1994. It wasn't something I was seeking. I had spent years rejecting mainstream Christianity, judging it to be riddled with hypocrisy and void of benefit for daily living. Still, I could no longer ignore my heart's cry for a divine relationship. I began attending a church that I cautiously viewed as spiritually legitimate.

One weekend, we had a guest minister. I remember enjoying his teaching and appreciating his warm, genuine, and witty personality. Though he spoke for several hours, I didn't mind. Listening to him, I became encouraged about developing a relationship with God. I became excited about what the future might hold.

As he finished his teaching, he announced his desire to individually pray for everyone present. I quickly scanned the sanctuary and estimated five hundred people in attendance. How could he pray for us individually, and why would he want to? It struck me as weird. I became further put off when people began streaming to the front of the sanctuary. Ushers organized them in a line that paralleled the stage and he went down the line, placing his hands on people's heads or shoulders, speaking what appeared to be quick prayers. Some of those he prayed for inexplicably fell backward, then were caught and eased to the floor by ushers.

At this point, my confusion turned to offense. This strange sight couldn't be God! I picked up my Bible preparing to leave. It was then I made one of the best decisions of my life but had no clue I was doing so. Instead of leaving, I decided I would go up front, get in the line, and have this obvious fraud pray for me. I knew that when he did, nothing would happen and that it would confirm the absence of God in this irreverent spectacle. I merged into the mass of people inching up the aisle, smug in the belief that I knew more about the ways of God than all the people around me. Talk about pride going before a fall!

Finally, I was in the prayer line up front. With a wide stance, hands clenched, and a rigid body, I determined to emerge unscathed from whatever he would do. Consumed with purpose, I lost all sense of those on either side of me. Suddenly he was in front of me. Looking at me with a peaceful but bemused demeanor, he placed his hand on my forehead. My body lurched back three feet, stopped only by an usher. Instantly, I felt unsteady and lightheaded. As he stepped forward, his eyes met mine and with a Louisiana drawl I will never forget, he forcefully said, "Son, the Lord wants to top off your tank." Bam! Lights out!

My next recollection resembles waking from a dream. Two men in blue blazers came into focus, their smiles wide and arms outstretched. Then it struck me: I'm not standing. I'm flat on my back! One of the men asked if I thought I could stand. Seeing my hesitant nod, they pulled me to my feet. Wobbly, I surveyed the area. People were lying everywhere, some laughing, some still as statues.

What had happened? I had no idea but I wasn't going to stick around to find out. I fled the sanctuary utterly bewildered.

The next morning, I awoke at my usual time. Heading to the shower, I became aware something was different. What was it? I paused and took a physical inventory. Somehow my body felt different. Wait! Where was the pain?

For years I had suffered from a chronic and agonizing back injury. It limited my mobility, made sleeping difficult, and left me depressed and irritable. My doctor said it would only get worse. It was a discouraging diagnosis for a man in his thirties.

That morning, after the previous night's encounter with the visiting minister, I felt no pain. There was no sign of injury. How could that be? I hadn't touched my toes in years and suddenly I was doing it with ease. I tried different stretches with the same result...no pain! My mind flashed to something I had said the night before.

While waiting in the prayer line, feeling only cynicism and disbelief, I had mockingly whispered to myself, "If this guy is really a man of God, I should have him pray for my back." My sarcastic implication was that I would only accept his legitimacy if he demonstrated a miracle of healing. No chance of that happening as I believed he was a fake. Besides, I had reasoned God is not interested in healing me or anyone else.

Now, stunned by the miracle that had occurred, I experienced an epiphany: When it came to understanding God, I was clueless! God obviously had heard my scornful comment. To my surprise, I hadn't offended Him. In fact, He had responded by healing me! Why would He do that?

That week, I bought my first book on healing. I bought more books and videos on healing in the months that followed. I attended healing conferences and sought out the teachings of ministries that had a healing emphasis. There was something about knowing God as my healer that captured my heart. I knew that what He had done for me, He would do for others. To see that happen became the passion of my life.

On January 1, 2000, I opened a healing center in Minneapolis, Minnesota. For the next three years, I had the privilege of witnessing miracles of every kind. Cancers disappeared, blind eyes regained vision, and injured bodies became whole. Witnessing God's love in action made it a wonderful time in my life. It cemented in my heart the knowledge that God desires to heal all who sincerely seeks Him.

Since then I have continued in ministry. I have pastored a church and taught and ministered healing in other churches. Time has served to strengthen my confidence in God's love. It has deepened my understanding of God's heart to heal every hurt, physical or otherwise.

My heart and soul were forever altered when God healed my body. I wrote this devotional because I passionately desire a similar experience for you. I pray for your physical healing and spiritual transformation. I also pray that your journey to wholeness yields an even greater blessing—the unmatched blessing of intimacy with God.

—Paul Richards

Utilizing the Prayers

In this book, each day's reading ends with a relevant prayer. The prayers are intentionally short and specific. Their effectiveness is determined not by their length, but by *how* they are prayed.

The Bible is different from all other books. Its words are "alive" (Heb 4:12), infused with the Holy Spirit. When we read, meditate on, and pray God's words, our spirits are nourished and developed as they absorb His truth. Faith is also a result of absorbing God's words. Faith can be defined as spiritual knowledge or revelation imparted by the Spirit of God. Romans 10:17 tells us that "faith comes by hearing, and hearing by the word of God."

Faith—or spiritual understanding—is essential for healing. Different from knowledge learned intellectually, faith or "belief" is purely spiritual. It is truth, God's truth, realized in our hearts. It enables us to "see" what is not visible in the physical world. It gives us confidence in God and reveals the spirit realm we share with Him. Faith for healing is the knowledge of, and belief in, God's healing power.

The prayers in this book are designed to build your faith. I encourage you to use them as meditations. Go through each one slowly, allowing for unhurried reading aloud and contemplation. For example, in the prayer for the first devotion, titled "God is Love," the first sentence is "Heavenly Father, I receive your love for me." Start by pondering just the first two words: "Heavenly Father." You can speak those words over and over, either in your mind or aloud, increasing your awareness of speaking directly to your Father in heaven. Consider that you have His undivided attention and that you are of infinite value to Him. Then, after a while, when you are ready, move on to "I receive your love for me." Repeat those words, letting them penetrate your heart and mind. "I receive your love...I receive your love...I receive your love..." Let those words fill you and strengthen your spirit. Doing this makes their truth *your* truth. Your faith will come alive, and with it, your ability to connect to God's healing power. You can then move on to the rest of the prayer at whatever pace you feel is right.

By taking your time with the teachings and prayers, you open your heart to God's grace and power. You also make yourself available to a relationship that goes beyond your physical needs—a relationship rooted in divine intimacy and love. Jesus went to the Cross to provide that for you. His sacrifice was complete and perfect, restoring to humanity all that was lost as a result of the Fall. I pray this devotional will be a resource that makes Christ and the Cross a reality in every part of your life.

Day 1

God is Love

God *is* love. Take a moment to consider that. Throughout the Bible, we are told God loves us, but in 1 John 4:8, 16 we are told that God *is* love. More than what He does, love is who and what He is. If you are in need of healing, understanding this reality is where your journey to wholeness begins.

For some, there is a tendency to believe He loves us only when we are doing "good." This produces the idea that God's love is conditional. It strikes to the core of our trust in God and keeps us unsure of our relationship with Him. How can we have faith He will heal us if we aren't even sure He loves us? Knowing God *as* love removes the lie of conditional love and gives us assurance that He always loves us—and that He always helps us.

Can you see why having a personal revelation of this is so important? Battling sickness is hard enough. Being sure of God's feelings toward us is critical to generating spiritual resistance to illness. If we understand that God loves because it is who He is and that He can't change (Mal 3:6), we can proceed knowing His effort on our behalf is guaranteed. When Satan tries to plant seeds of doubt concerning God's commitment to our lives, we can confidently dismiss those lies as contrary to God's nature and character. Receiving His love frees us from anxiety about being healed and centers our hearts on His loyalty to our lives.

So take comfort in knowing that God's love for you is continuous. Rejoice that He loves you no matter what you say or do. Live confidently and joyfully in the knowledge and light of His adoration. Above all, have faith that God's love for you is stronger than any sickness and that love never fails (1 Cor 13:8)!

Prayer

Heavenly Father, I receive your love for me. I believe it is given freely and unconditionally. Because you are love and because love never fails, I believe you are healing me as I pray. It is my joy and privilege to love you in return. Amen.

Day 2

God's Gift for You

"Heal the sick...freely you have received, freely give" (Matt 10:8). These wonderful words of instruction, given by Jesus to His disciples, reveal more than their simple directive would imply.

With a few words, Jesus made clear His desire to heal and defined healing as a gift to be received by all. Notice how inclusive His words are. No one is excluded. No one is denied.

For some, this is hard to accept. They believe healing could never be a free gift, that there is something we must do to receive it. The more cynical or skeptical take it further, speculating that seeking God for healing is a way for Him to intrude in our lives, to gain control. After all, if something seems too good to be true, it probably is, right?

Not with God! Remember, He already proved His willingness to give freely, and it was with something more valuable than healing. Romans 8:32 states: "He who did not spare His own Son, but delivered Him up for us all, how shall He not with Him also freely give us all things?" Does it make sense that He would give us His most precious possession, without our even asking, but say no to something of lesser value? Of course not. If He did, He would be placing a greater value on the gift of healing than on the sacrifice of His own Son.

God's willingness to heal is just one aspect of His heart for us. By sending His Son, He made a way for every part of our lives—spirit, soul, and body—to be restored by Him. The work of the Cross is all-encompassing; it leaves no part of life untouched. Receiving healing is no different from receiving salvation—it is the acceptance of a gift already given.

Choose to receive God's free gift of healing. Recognize God's desire to bless you, just as He did with an even greater gift—the gift of His Son.

Prayer

Lord, with gratitude I accept your gift of healing. Thank you for ministering to my body even now. I receive the fullness of your power in every area of need. Amen.

Day 3

Healing in the Word

The Bible is a mystical book. Authored by the creator of the universe, its words are infused with His spirit. At a glance, it may look like any other book, but that is where the comparison ends.

Think of its unique power! When we read it with an open heart, it reveals God's nature and character. It transforms us into His image, it builds faith and hope, and it imparts peace and comfort.

For those in need of healing, meditating and praying healing scriptures links us directly to God's restorative power. Just by reading or hearing God's word, our faith and our capacity to receive from God are strengthened (Rom 10:17).

God promises that His word, which is truth, will make us free (Jn 8:32). Some years ago, I developed painful skin blisters. The doctors I saw could not explain their cause nor offer helpful treatment. Needing relief from this condition, I decided to put God's word to the test. I settled on Isaiah 53:5 "…by His stripes I am healed." This was the healing scripture I would meditate on, ponder and pray, for the next six months. During that time, nothing changed physically, but my faith grew. One afternoon, as I was beginning my prayer time, the power of God hit me like a lightning bolt. In that moment, the truth of Isaiah 53:5 became real in a way that I can only describe as supernatural. I knew instantly that God's word was true and that I was healed. Within hours, every blister was gone, never to return!

What had happened? Simply put, supernatural revelation of God's word, developed through prayer and meditation, created a supernatural healing connection. Truth—God's truth—made me free.

Right now, that same connection is available to you. Please take time to choose a scripture, or scriptures, that you will make your own. They are your personal links to God and the wholeness you seek. Pray them, receive them, meditate on them. This is God's medicine at its best!

Prayer

Father, I thank you for your word. I ask for your direction to scriptures that will bring revelation to my life. By your spirit, teach me to meditate on them and receive healing from them. Thank you, Lord. Amen.

Day 4

Faith

Faith. A word big enough to be its own sentence. Entire ministries have been dedicated to teaching about it and about how to make it real in our lives. Countless books have been written trying to define it. However complex it may seem, Jesus taught that faith is simple—something that can be understood by all.

Why, then, is faith viewed as such a complex subject? Probably because it has a place of prominence in the Bible. That prominence generates theological interest and study. Unfortunately, its importance provokes an attempt to define intellectually what can only be understood with the assistance of the Holy Spirit. Remember, Jesus said His words are "spirit and they are life" (Jn 6:63) and, as stated by the apostle Paul, can only be "spiritually discerned" (1 Cor 2:14). We make faith (and every other Biblical concept) complicated—even incomprehensible—when we explore it without His assistance.

God never intended this. He gave us the aid of the Holy Spirit to comprehend His word and to prevent erroneous interpretations. He wants faith to be part of who we are, not something to be understood only in theory.

Let's follow the lead of Jesus and keep it simple. He taught that faith is something a child demonstrates—a pure and innocent trusting of the heart (Lk 18:15-18). To operate in faith, we need only to believe in the truth of what God has said. It's that easy! Believing God has provided healing through the Cross is faith at its finest, and it is all the faith you need to receive your healing.

If you can do that, you're good to go. Don't let anything or anyone make it more complicated. Declare that Christ died so that you can be healed. Take ownership of what He has done for you. Accept the truth of healing as *your* truth. Receive it, absorb it, and treat it as the precious, blood-bought, life-giving gift it is! Do that and you won't have to understand faith. It will become part of who you are!

Prayer

Lord, I declare my faith to be pure and powerful. Thank you for making faith part of my being. I believe in your gift of healing and receive healing in return. Amen.

Day 5

Hope

Sometimes asking a question is as important as the answer it may provide. That said, let me ask you a simple one. Are you *sincerely* expecting to be healed? Be honest. In the depths of your heart, are you convinced that you will be made whole? It is fine if you aren't sure. Some people don't even know they can expect to be healed. But here is an interesting fact: God expects us to expect it, and that expectation is called hope!

In our modern culture, hoping for something is often synonymous with *wishing* for something, such as, "I wish I had more money" or "I wish I were married." Not so with the Bible. Scripture defines hope as an earnest or confident expectation to experience that which is desired. Furthermore, Scripture tells us that it is God himself who supernaturally gives us the ability to hope for—or expect—His blessing in our lives (Rom 15:13).

Hope is a supernatural force that works with our faith to bring about what we want or need. If you aren't sure of the difference between faith and hope, think of it this way: Faith is the understanding that something exists (such as healing for our bodies), and hope is the expectation to see it. Can you see how they work together? Faith recognizes what God has provided for us, and hope is the confidence to see it come to pass.

Don't be discouraged if you are low on hope. God is available right now to give you more—just ask! Remember, as His child, you have every right to expect His blessings. That isn't being presumptuous. It's what God desires (Jn 14:13)!

The author of Hebrews wrote: "Let us hold fast the confession of our hope without wavering, for He who promised is faithful" (Heb 10:23). This makes clear our hope is in God and in His faithfulness to us. We never need to doubt His intentions toward us. Instead, we can expect His best for our lives—and that is something to hope for!

Prayer

Lord, with great expectation I look to you for healing. My hope and faith are rooted in your love for me and the work of the Cross. With thanksgiving I receive the manifestation of my expectation. In the name of Jesus I pray. Amen.

Day 6

Identity

It has been said that we are what we eat (though this may mean I am a Mexican restaurant). Interestingly, the Bible makes a similar but more accurate point: We are (and become) what we believe we are (Prov 23:7). Seeing ourselves healed, or "identifying" with being healed, connects us to healing and helps us become whole.

As human beings we tend to identify ourselves in specific ways: I am happy. I am sad. I am wealthy. I am poor. I am healthy. I am sick. Even if they are not entirely accurate to begin with, over time such definitive statements become self-fulfilling. We become what we believe we are!

Knowing this, it is important to never identify with the sickness that has come against your body. Don't "own" or make part of your identity that from which you want to be free. Don't say, "I am sick" or "I am a diabetic" or "I have cancer." That is taking ownership and making those things part of how you see yourself—your identity. That seals those things both spiritually and physically to your life. It is more spiritually accurate—and better for you—to say, "I'm fighting sickness" or "I'm battling diabetes" or "I'm resisting cancer." By making the distinction, you don't undermine your faith that you will be healed. Instead, you keep an accurate perspective on sickness and its opposition to God's plan for your life.

When battling sickness or any other negative situation, it is critical to focus on your true identity—your identity in Christ. If you are not sure of what that means—or looks like—think of how you see Jesus. Do you see Him as holy, righteous, untouchable from any work of darkness, including sickness? As hard as it may be to believe, that is how God sees you, and how He wants you to see yourself (Col 1:13, 22). Viewing yourself as God sees you—taking ownership of your life in a spiritual way—separates you from the force of darkness and activates your connection to Him. That is something we all can identify with!

Prayer

Father, I resolve today to see myself as you see me. I see myself as healed and whole, loved and adored. I praise and thank you for making this a reality in my life! Amen.

Day 7

Make a Connection

At its core, healing is about connection—Divine connection. From creation, God intended that we live connected to His very being, drawing on that union for the fulfillment of every need, including healing.

For centuries, humanity has struggled to grasp the connection He offers. Sadly, some religions teach that God is distant and uninterested in the lives of humans. It stretches the imagination to consider He is always available, offering unrestricted access to Himself, holding nothing back (Rom 8:32). Yet that is the truth, and when we complicate the simplicity of this, we hinder our ability to connect with His power.

Think of how you receive a gift. When it is handed to you, are you thinking you need to pay for it, that you don't deserve it, that you have to offer a gift in return? No! It's a gift, right? You receive it with gratitude and excitement. You recognize that reciprocity isn't expected or desired.

This is the attitude and perspective we are to display in connecting with—and receiving from—Him. Connecting to the healing power of God is simply yielding to that which already exists—that to which we are already joined. *Because God is always present, His healing power is always present.* We don't have to convince Him to release it, we don't have to persuade Him of our worthiness to receive it, we don't have to wonder if He will help us. Our only action should be yielding with gratitude to what He is giving so freely.

Decide today to let nothing interfere with your connection to God. Determine to keep your relationship with Him the perfect union He created it to be. Live from that place and you will always be connected!

Prayer

Heavenly Father, I thank you that I am divinely connected. I yield to the power of that connection, receiving healing in my body, even now as I pray. With faith and thanksgiving, I receive the blessing of our union. Thank you, Lord. Amen.

Day 8

See the Goal

I am an avid dirt-bike rider. I have learned when riding that it is important to look far ahead, focusing on the best course to take—not on the immediate obstacles covering the trail. This is necessary because you subconsciously steer toward what you fixate on. Focus on an impediment in your path and you will strike it. At high rates of speed, through hazard packed trails, you need discipline to ignore obstructions and concentrate on the safest line. In doing so, something amazing happens: You and your bike go exactly where you are looking. It is almost as if you are steering only with your eyes.

This is an interesting physiological phenomenon but it also reflects a spiritual principle. When pursuing a kingdom blessing, such as healing, disciplined, forward-looking focus is essential to its realization. Specifically, this means concentrating only on the desired outcome and not on things that discourage you from obtaining it.

Let's say we are dealing with a serious medical issue. These usually come with associated challenges, including responsibilities regarding family, employment, relationships, or commitments. Illness can take heavy emotional tolls. It can leave us exhausted and depressed. Increased stress levels become a factor both for us and those around us. If not addressed, the medical challenge, serious enough on its own, can become part of larger, even more debilitating dynamic.

This is where placing our focus on the promise of God is critical. *Resisting distractions, we have to see with our hearts—and our mind's eye—the manifestation of God's healing power.* We have to choose to believe, trust, and expect God's faithful response. While not ignoring responsibilities, we can't allow them to cloud our focus.

Peter walked on water as long as his eyes were on Jesus; he sank when he focused on the stormy waves (Matt 14:30). Your path to healing is found by fixating on Jesus, letting your focus on Him steer you to wholeness. You can be confident that is exactly what will happen!

Prayer

God, I choose to make you the focus of my life. I resolve to filter all efforts and decisions through the wisdom and love of your Holy Spirit. Because I do, I believe you will guide me to blessing and wholeness. Amen.

Day 9

The Spiritual vs. The Natural

The Word tells us that healing is a finished work—something God makes available without restriction (1 Pet 2:24, Matt 10:7). For many, this raises obvious questions. If the work of healing is finished, why am I sick? If I *was* healed, why is there a delay in its manifestation? Good questions but the answers have regrettably been muddied by misconceptions and bad doctrine. Some well-intentioned believers go so far as to teach that sickness can't be acknowledged, that doing so gives potency to the sickness, demonstrates a lack of faith, and insults the work of the Cross.

This kind of doctrinal debate is unnecessary and harmful. It is also a waste of time and energy. We can acknowledge the assault of sickness on our lives while still recognizing God's supremacy over all things, including illness.

The natural world in which we live is a fallen one—a world influenced by Satan, sin, and immorality. We live in this world and must deal with its dark forces. Yet, as believers, we also dwell in the spiritual kingdom of God. Being in this realm has tremendous rewards, including access to a power far greater than that of the natural world. When sickness comes against our bodies, we can lay hold of that supernatural power and, by faith, experience deliverance and healing.

Let me give an illustration that I hope will make things clearer. Think of the law of gravity. It is an established fact. Drop a ball and it falls to the ground. Yet there is a force that overcomes the fact, or law, of gravity. A higher truth, if you will. The force of flight, observed every day in birds and airplanes, routinely overcome the force of gravity. Sickness, like gravity, may be a fact of life, but God's healing power—a higher truth—can overcome sickness with the ease of a bird taking wing.

Prayer

Lord, I thank you for delivering me from the forces of darkness and placing me in your family and kingdom (Col 1:13). I receive the blessings and benefits of being your child, including healing for my body. In your precious name I pray. Amen.

Day 10

Love Yourself

Years ago, during a time of personal reflection, I realized something painful and profound. I was living with a lack of forgiveness—not toward others, but toward myself. In addition, I was living without self-acceptance. I didn't like myself, and I certainly didn't love myself.

On the list of things we consider essential to daily living, accepting and loving ourselves may not even register. Our hurried lifestyles offer little time for personal reflection. Besides, being self-affirming strikes many as being self-absorbed. And what does it have to do with getting healed?

These are valid questions but they miss the point. Love is the river on which God's blessings flow. Love for Him, love for self, love for others. These things are foundational to living as God intends (Mk 12:30-31). In addition, an inability to love and accept oneself points to issues that have to be resolved regardless of one's need for physical healing. It reveals brokenness in the soul, which is as much a priority for healing as anything else.

The Apostle John wrote, "Beloved, I pray that you may prosper in all things and be in health, just as your soul prospers" (3 Jn 2). Please note he ties good health to a thriving soul. Living without love and self-acceptance severs the bond between body and soul—it short-circuits the harmony essential to connecting with God.

If you have struggled with insecurity, self-rejection, or self-condemnation, begin the journey to wholeness by focusing on God's love for you, not on your perceived faults or mistakes. Acknowledge that you are accepted and adored by a God unmoved by your shortcomings. Work on self-improvement when possible, but do so through the filter of God's overwhelming love for you.

When I fully accepted His love for me, I was able to accept and love myself. It opened a floodgate of healing in my life and it will do the same for you. Choose to love yourself because *He* loves you. You don't need any other reason than that!

Prayer

Heavenly Father, in the name of your Son Jesus, I accept the fullness of your love for me. I declare I am worthy of your love, and I choose to accept and love myself unconditionally. Amen.

Day 11

Healing Is a Finished Work

I Peter 2:24 declares, "...by His stripes you *were* healed" (emphasis added). He refers to God's work of healing in the past tense because, through Christ's crucifixion, it is complete. Everything necessary for you to be made whole has been accomplished through Christ and released by the Holy Spirit.

A revelation of this truth should produce immense relief and gratitude. It also should put to rest the idea that in order to receive healing from God, we need to work up something ourselves. Obtaining healing should never be thought of as a formula to be followed or a puzzle to be solved. Connecting to God's healing power isn't a goal we strive for but a gift we receive.

Consider 2 Corinthians 1:20. It states that God has already answered yes (past tense again) to any requests we make, as they relate to His promises to us. Be it a need for healing or anything else, if it is in line with His word, He has already approved our request (Jn 15:7, 1 Jn 5:14-15).

This raises an interesting question. If God has already said yes to our request for healing, do we need to ask Him to heal us? Think about it. Do you ask for permission to drive your car or enter your home? Of course not. They belong to you. The same can be said of healing. His Word makes clear it is our covenant right—our inheritance. In a sense, asking Him to heal us implies God is undecided about healing us. This contradicts His declaration that He *has* healed us.

I point this out not to split doctrinal hairs but to keep our faith focused on an established Biblical truth. God *has* released His healing power and He *has* said yes to our requests to receive it. Instead of asking Him to do something now, why not receive what He has already done?

Prayer

God, I thank you for the provision of healing. Right now, in the name of your son Jesus, I receive your gift of healing to my body. I receive it freely and with gratitude. Thank you. Amen.

Day 12

Single-Mindedness

In overcoming sickness, it is important to keep your mind free of fearful and discouraging thoughts. This can be difficult because the pain and fatigue affecting our bodies also wearies our minds. A tired mind is far more susceptible to the depressing thoughts Satan sends our way.

Why is Satan so persistent in attacking our thoughts? Because in doing so, he seeks to create what the apostle James called "double-mindedness" (Jas 1:8). This is a harmful spiritual condition that hinders us from manifesting the healing power of God. Let's look at James 1, starting with verse 5, to better understand:

> *If any of you lacks wisdom, let him ask of God, who gives to all liberally and without reproach, and it will be given to him. But let him ask in faith, with no doubting, for he who doubts is like a wave of the sea driven and tossed by the wind. For let not that man suppose that he will receive anything from the Lord; he is a double-minded man ...*

Please read this carefully, considering two essential points. First, though the writer is referencing wisdom, anything we need from God could be substituted for wisdom, such as healing, provision or peace. The principle is the same as it all comes from the work of the Cross. Whatever we lack, we can ask of God and He will give generously.

Second—and this is key—James is not implying that God withholds from someone who doubts or is "double-minded" because He is displeased. God never withholds. He has already said yes (2 Cor 1:20) to anything asked according to His word. Rather, doubt-producing thoughts and words directed at us from Satan can hinder *our* abilities to receive what God has already provided. Think of negative and discouraging thoughts as things that harm your capacity to receive, not God's ability to give.

Guarding the mind is critical to keeping our faith connection with God. Choose to resist dark thoughts. Be singular of mind in trusting God and you will never restrict His power in your life.

Prayer

God, I choose to keep my focus on you.
I reject discouraging thoughts. By your
grace, my outlook is hopeful and my faith
undeterred. Amen.

Day 13

Thought Life

In yesterday's devotion we emphasized resisting dark and discouraging thoughts. For many, living with worrisome and anxiety-producing thoughts is normal. Some even embrace a pessimistic attitude, identifying with a negative view of life. I have heard people declare such things as "I'm a worrier; it's who I am" or "bad things always happen to me."

This view of life is damaging in various ways. Because it contradicts God's heart and plan for our lives, it hinders the connection of our faith to the power of God. It stands in opposition to what God has promised and forges an agreement with Satan's harmful efforts.

However, by recognizing and opposing these destructive lies (2 Cor 10:5), we can limit their effects by renewing our minds (Rom 12:2) with Scripture. This means we replace negative thoughts with positive ones. More specifically, we replace the lies of the devil with the promises of God.

In the long term, the best way to develop and maintain a peaceful and profitable thought life is to follow the advice found in the book of Philippians. Verse 6 of chapter 4 tells us: "Do not be anxious about anything..." and verses 8 and 9 tell us to think only about those things which are "...true... pure...lovely...praiseworthy..."*

This may sound unrealistic, impractical, and even impossible. But remember, God wouldn't direct us to do something without making it possible for us to succeed.

I recommend starting with small but consistent steps. For instance, throughout the day, pause for a minute or two and contemplate something encouraging. If the illness you are fighting is causing stress, meditate on scriptures referencing God's healing power. Remind yourself of all the things you are grateful for—even make a list if it will help. Commit to having a positive attitude, regardless of circumstances. Do this and a peaceful and blessed thought life can be yours.

Prayer

Lord, I thank you for a mind that thinks
as you do (1 Cor 2:16). I accept your
help to remain peaceful and positive in
my thoughts. With gratitude, I receive the
blessings that flow from this divine place.
Amen.

*NIV Translation

Day 14

Speak It Out

When a magician performs an illusion, just prior to its flashy conclusion, he or she usually says something intended to sound mystical, such as "Abracadabra!" By speaking those "enchanted" words, something unseen is supposed to appear (think rabbit from a hat).

Interestingly, the notion of speaking words to make something appear is scriptural. Think of the way God created the world. He *spoke* it into existence. Romans 4:17 declares: "God…calls those things which do not exist as though they did." God speaks and it happens!

As you proceed in your journey of healing, speaking faith-filled words over your life is essential. Examples of these scripture-based declarations could include, "By Christ's sacrifice I am whole" or "I have been delivered from sickness and disease—I am free!"

At first, making these kinds of statements may seem odd, even ridiculous. After all, isn't doing so denying the reality of the situation? Not really. It is choosing to place one's faith and focus on something more powerful than sickness—a supernatural reality that trumps the force of illness. By speaking affirming words—from the heart—we connect to the supernatural and release its power into our lives.

Years ago I experienced a painful injury. Even slight movement produced wrenching spasms. One day as I was trying to get dressed, the pain became so great I collapsed on the bed. A righteous anger arose at this agonizing predicament and I began to declare, "I am healed in the name of Jesus!" To anyone observing, I would have looked delusional. I was obviously incapacitated, yet I was almost shouting words to the contrary.

What happened next? God's power flooded my body with such force that I was immediately pain free and injury free. Imagine if I had stopped just seconds sooner, thinking my words silly and futile. I could have missed my connection to healing and spent days recuperating without spiritual support.

2 Corinthians 5:7 states, "For we walk [live] by faith, not by sight." Speak words of higher truth and you can have your own "Abracadabra" moment—only it will be real, never an illusion!

Prayer

Father, as your child I live by faith. By your grace, my words have miraculous power. I speak healing to my body and expect it to occur. Amen.

Day 15

Communion

The principles of God's kingdom are simple by design. Available to all, they have countless benefits but one overriding purpose: to direct people to God.

Communion is no exception. Given by God as an experiential reminder of Christ's sacrifice and the benefits His atonement provides, communion unites us with the essence of the Cross. When we partake with understanding and faith, God's healing power is supernaturally imparted. For someone battling an illness, the daily taking of communion is highly recommended.

If you have never taken communion outside of church, or never taken it at all, don't be concerned. I will walk you through it.

Start by gathering the bread and wine (sometimes referred to as "the elements"). No bread or wine? No problem. You can use Pepsi and a potato chip or tea and a cracker. It doesn't matter. Whatever you have handy is fine.

Now quiet your thoughts. Begin to reflect on the work of the Cross. Personalize it. Imagine Jesus going to the Cross with you on His mind. Take the bread. It represents His body broken for you. As you eat it, see the beating He received. See Him absorbing the power of sin, of sickness, of disease. His acceptance of this horror, and His subsequent resurrection, is what breaks the power of the affliction warring against you. Receive His sacrifice for you and simultaneously reject the power of sickness to harm you. Don't pay in your body what He paid for in His!

Finish by drinking the wine—it symbolizes His blood. Thank Him for shedding it. In doing so, He removed the judgment we deserved for our sins and paid for that judgment Himself. His spilled blood also bought us unrestricted access to God.

In conclusion, take communion whenever you can. It is an effective way to connect with God's healing power—the best medicine of all!

Prayer

(Before you pray, gather the elements).

Lord, I honor your body, which was broken to destroy the power of sin, sickness, and disease. I eat this bread believing that the power of illness is removed from my body. I drink this wine acknowledging your blood bought my freedom from eternal judgment for sin, and brought me into perfect union with you. Thank you, Jesus. Amen.

Day 16

The Power of Peace

What facilitates healing, protects us, and enriches every aspect of living? Winning the lottery? Maybe, but even more potent than wealth is something God gives, something material resources can't provide. It is the peace of God. It has no equal in its life-enhancing capability.

We don't often think of peace as inherently dynamic—even aggressive—in its function. To many, peace is passive; it invokes the image of submission or compliance. But where is the strength in that? How can peace resist, let alone overcome, something as destructive as disease?

To better understand the power of peace, let's review its Biblical definition. As it is conveyed in the Hebrew text, peace (or shalom) signifies more than tranquility or absence of conflict. It refers to good health, prosperity, completeness—the well-being of the total person. In its purest sense, peace is a fearless state of being, reflecting God's life combined with ours.

Can you see how this supernatural assurance, this God-infused confidence, deters and repels efforts contrary to God's design? A person at peace is a person convinced of his or her security and wholeness in Christ. This certainty—this belief—rebuffs demonic aggression. It exposes the inferiority of Satan's endeavors. It enables us to see life as God sees it and, rest assured, God is at peace.

Personally, I am diligently protective of the peace God has granted me. I avoid dynamics that challenge it, such as pointless conflict or unhealthy relationships. When a difficult circumstance arises, particularly of a demonic nature (such as illness), I remind myself that if it can't steal my peace, it can't succeed against me. I trust in the divine attributes of peace and its capacity to defeat all efforts of darkness. I remind myself that peace comes from God to reassure and protect. I trust in Paul's prayer from 2 Thessalonians 3:16 which states "…the Lord of peace Himself give you peace always in every way." I trust in that for you as well.

Prayer

Lord, I thank you for giving me your peace.
I receive its comfort, its protection, and
its healing power. I ask for its continual
operation in every part of my life. Amen.

∽

Day 17

When, God? When?

Healing is about connection—supernatural connection that allows God's power to touch our bodies and remove illness.

There are things we can do to facilitate that connection—things like meditating on His word, speaking and praying scripture-based affirmations, avoiding stress, and receiving healing-prayer. These positive actions are helpful, even necessary. Think of them as components that create a lifestyle for manifesting healing.

This brings us to the question of *when* to expect healing to occur. I wish I could give you a specific answer, but that would imply that healing comes by formula—not by faith—which would involve taking our eyes off of God and placing them on a quantifiable process.

It is perfectly natural to wonder about the timing of healing, as well as to ponder how to make it happen faster. Unfortunately, these thoughts can send us searching for shortcuts to quicken the process. They can also cause us to question God's love and commitment to our well-being.

Fixating on *when* our healing will occur can cause us to lose sight of a critical truth. God, through the Cross, has already released His spirit of healing into the world. We don't need to convince Him to heal us. Instead, we are seeking to connect with what He has already made available. Connecting to this is dependent on our believing it exists—it has nothing to do with saying or doing the right things to provoke a response from God. He has already said yes!

The next time you find yourself becoming fixated on the "when" of your healing, remind yourself that the "when" occurred two thousand years ago. Direct your attention to this and instead of saying, "When, God? When?" you will find yourself saying, "I receive, God. I receive."

Prayer

Father, I believe in the finished work of your Son and my Lord, Jesus Christ. By faith I connect with your healing power, available to me right now. I receive all that I need for health and wholeness. Thank you, Lord. Amen.

Day 18

Confidence Before God

Consider this: The most significant event in your life occurred before you were even born. Your life's second most influential event also occurred prior to your birth. They are respectively the work of the Cross, some two thousand years ago, and the fall of humanity, about six thousand years ago.

The first needed to occur because of the second. The fall allowed demonic darkness, with its destructive results, into life on earth. Even worse, our perfect union with God was lost.

Christ came to redeem and restore. He came to reset that connection and empower us to live supernaturally bonded to Him. Confidence in our relationship with Him requires our understanding of this. We have to know there is nothing wrong between us and God, or our faith simply won't work.

What Jesus did was a perfect work. Through the Cross, He brought us into unrestricted union with God (Gal 2:20, Jn 14:20), guaranteeing that never again will we have to feel unworthy or ashamed in His presence. Consider Ephesians 3:12, which states: "...we have *boldness* and access [to Him] with *confidence*..." or Hebrews 4:16, which implores us to "... come *boldly* to the throne of grace that we may obtain mercy and find grace to help in time of need." [Emphasis added.]

God desires—and even expects—us to live confidently in our relationship with Him. That idea can be hard to accept, even intimidating. For many, living confidently in personal and professional relationships is difficult enough. But when we understand God's love for us and our union with Him, we will be more at ease with Him than with anyone else.

Remember, He wouldn't have made a perfect relationship possible if He didn't want one...with you! It is that glorious union, free of shame or insecurity, that paves the way for everything we need, including our healing. Live confidently before God and expect His best in your life. You both will be glad you did!

Prayer

Lord, I thank you for my perfect union
with you. Because of it, I live confidently
and expectantly in your presence. I declare
nothing separates me from you or your
healing power. Amen.

Day 19

Confidence in God

When it comes to our health, where do we place our trust? Doctors and medicine? Exercise, nutrition, good sleep, meditation? There is nothing wrong with these things—quite the contrary—but it is interesting to note that the list doesn't include God. For many that makes sense. Even for those in a relationship with God, considering Him as a source for health and healing can seem misguided.

This is a shame because no one knows us the way God knows us. He is conscious of every part of our being, from the inside out. He has no constraints when it comes to healing. How odd to suppose that the One who created us is not capable of healing us, or at least not interested in doing so.

Ministering in Africa taught me firsthand what confidence in God can produce. In remote villages, where health care is scarce—and unaffordable for many—being healed by God is the only hope for most people, their only path to wellness. This dependency on God, and the expectation He will heal, is often unshakeable. The results are miracles, staggering in both power and number. I have been privileged to witness terminal illnesses and severe impairments such as blindness and deafness be healed in an instant. I have seen those types of miracles in prosperous nations as well. Still, it is apparent a confidence born out of necessity can generate a potent connection to God's healing power.

I share this not to dissuade anyone from available treatment. Rather, my hope is that God will be included—confidently—into a program of medical treatment. Jesus never turned away anyone who sought Him for healing (Matt 15:30, 31). Time and again, He demonstrated God's heart for the hurting. This same Jesus remains unchanged in His desire to heal you. You can be assured of this truth. You can trust in His miraculous power. Most important, you can be confident in Him!

Prayer

*Lord, I thank you for your faithfulness
to me. I am grateful for your willingness
to minister to every part of my life. I
confidently look and listen for your
direction. I expectantly receive your
healing touch. Amen.*

Day 20

Be Proactive

Does God need our help? Could we help Him if we tried? Odd as it is sounds, the answer to both those questions is yes. He has called us—and He counts on us—to share the truth of salvation through his son Jesus. Referred to as the Great Commission (Matt 28:16-20), the Bible makes clear that we can assist God by sharing His love with others.

What about on a more personal level? Can we help God help us? Specifically, are there things we can do to assist in receiving our healing from God? Again, the answer is yes. By cooperating with a variety of kingdom principles, we help facilitate the best possible connection to His healing power. Let's look at some examples of how we can be proactive.

Perhaps the best place to start is with love. The Bible makes it clear that there is no greater power and that even our faith works by love (1 Cor 13:8, Gal 5:6). Choosing to love in all circumstances, no matter how difficult, prevents the formation of barriers that stop us from receiving the fullness of His touch. Deciding to live in peace, to be merciful and forgiving, is also beneficial. Rejecting offense, bitterness, envy, and judgmental behavior is important as well. These actions require our effort but pay off in an unhindered union with Him.

Besides addressing internal issues, we can also attend to the external things that comprise our daily living. For instance, I have found that creating an atmosphere of praise and worship, whether at home, in the car, or even at work, produces great results in staying connected to God's power and peace. When feasible, I avoid people, places, or things that I know are working against the righteous structure of God's kingdom. I seek to protect the positive in my life, knowing that doing so is conducive to keeping God's manifest presence active. I am proactive because, by His grace, the benefits always outweigh the effort.

Prayer

God, I choose to be proactive in living my
life for you. I ask for your grace to live as you
live, free of all things negative or destructive.
I cooperate with your plan for my life and
your power to make it happen. Amen.

Day 21

Fear

As faith connects us to God, fear connects us to darkness. 1 John 4:18 tells us that fear is harmful—it damages our spirits, souls, and bodies. Fear is one of Satan's primary weapons against humanity. No one knows this better than someone battling a serious or life-threatening illness. Fear can be an overwhelming force, unrelenting in its assault.

If you are facing fear, you are not alone. You may feel isolated, even abandoned, but that is just part of Satan's strategy. At its core, fear is a lie. It is Satan's effort to make a lie a reality. He offers bad news but we should never accept it as true.

The good news is that God provides a way to overcome fear. It is love—God's love—and there is nothing else like it. He pours it out unceasingly, directing it at every part of our lives. When we yield to love, embracing it and reveling in it, fear is stripped of its power. Focusing on love and absorbing its strength turns fear back on Satan and drives him away.

Fear cannot exist in the presence of God's love. As light dispels darkness, love scatters fear. Fear cannot hurt us, nor fulfill its purpose, if we deny its truth and counter it with love. By ignoring its threats, by rejecting its intimidation, we render it powerless. The only strength that fear has is that which we give it—when we agree with its lies.

One of the best ways to develop love's protective power is to meditate on the ways God shows His love. Think of His love for you personally, ponder His promises, and consider His desire to bless every area of your life. Contemplate what you mean to God. Consider that the Father, Son, and Holy Spirit give you their continuous undivided attention—because they love you!

By keeping a steady focus on God's love for you and on His constant effort on your behalf (Rom 8:27, 34), fear will have little chance to succeed.

Prayer

Lord, I reject the lies of fear. I reject fear's right to operate in my life. I place my focus on you and your love for me. Thank you for driving fear away and strengthening me with your peace and love. Amen.

Day 22

God and Doctors

Over the years, I have received many questions about the relationship between healing through faith and healing through medicine. Some denominations or streams of ministry have taught that the two are incompatible, stating that seeking treatment from doctors reveals a lack of faith in God. In a few tragic cases, these rigid beliefs have led to unnecessary loss of life. However unintentional, these strict ideas ignore a critical truth: Both God and doctors desire the same outcome—the healing of illness.

While it is understandable to want healing from God—and Him alone—wisdom dictates prudent flexibility in conquering illness or injury.

The body of Christ is regrettably divided on this subject. I have had people tell me that God is not interested in healing them or anyone else, and they wouldn't presume to waste His time asking for help. Still others have stated that going to a doctor is sinful because Christians are to live by faith and faith alone.

Both positions are extreme and unscriptural. The key is to seek God while learning about, then applying, helpful treatment options. Ask for His assistance in connecting with the right doctors, therapy, or medicines. Remember, sickness is of the enemy. Anything that fights it is a good thing! Utilize every resource you can in driving it from your life. God wants you to be well. Let Him help by welcoming Him into your journey to wholeness.

If you are a new believer or someone struggling to hear the voice of God, it may seem daunting to seek His direction for healing. Don't be discouraged! Keep your peace and seek out the prayer support of mature brothers and sisters in the Lord. Pray with those who believe in God's healing power and who can help you discern the Lord's direction. Trust in the goodness of God. The path to healing is different for all, but God's intended outcome will always be the same!

Prayer

Lord, I look to you for direction. I trust you to guide my decision making. I believe you are leading me into a place of perfect health and wholeness. Thank you, God. Amen.

Day 23

Thanksgiving

Great pain and destruction came to a church I once attended, when its pastor admitted to an affair. He stepped down from ministry and separated from his wife. I ran into her months later. We talked a bit and I felt led to ask if she had identified what she believed had caused his hurtful behavior. Her answer not only amazed me, it changed my life. She replied sadly: "He wasn't thankful for what he had, and that made it much easier to do what he knew was wrong."

It took a few days of prayer to absorb what she had said. God then revealed a life-altering truth. An attitude of gratitude—of genuine thanksgiving—is not simply an appropriate social response to another person's kind or generous action. It is a *supernatural* force—a place of strength from which we can live. Gratitude to God, appreciation for our family and friends, and thankfulness for the biggest and smallest of blessings, elevates us above demonic enticements. It gives an accurate view of life's purpose and priorities.

Challenges are abundant when dealing with illness. Keeping a positive attitude, let alone a grateful one, may seem unrealistic. However, if attention is given to what we treasure, if we keep our hearts and minds focused on the positive, we greatly reduce our susceptibility to forces of darkness. Even illness-induced emotions, such as discouragement and self-pity, depart from the force of a thankful spirit.

Give it a try right now. If it helps, make a list of everything for which you are grateful. Choose a few and start thanking God for them. This will stir your heart and begin lifting you above negative emotions. From there, think of the memories most precious to you. Then, think of what you desire to experience in the future. Allow yourself to get excited about your future and start thanking God for the blessings He has in store. Let yourself see and feel those things that touch your heart the most.

Embrace the proverbial "attitude of gratitude" on a daily basis. You will be thankful you did!

Prayer

Heavenly Father, I express my gratitude for all of your blessings, both large and small. I choose to live thankfully, believing for your best in every part of my life. Amen.

Day 24

A Good Kind of Stubborn

Sometimes illness or injury is so severe that medical assistance offers no path to recovery.

I met a man whose wife suffered a major stroke. Doctors pronounced her brain-damaged and likely to die in a matter of days. When her husband Ken prayed, he heard God say: "She will live and not die and declare the works of the Lord" (an almost verbatim rendering of Ps 118:17). Ken said that those words exploded in his spirit and he knew if didn't let go of them—if he hung on to them no matter what the doctors said—his wife, Ellen, would recover.

Days turned to weeks and though Ellen remained alive in a coma, there was no physical improvement. Ken continued to profess and pray, sometimes for hours a day, that Ellen would live and not die. Initially, he received a lot of prayer support from family and friends, but that waned as Ellen's condition continued unchanged. Eventually, Ken was the only one who believed she would recover.

It was then that Ken experienced something unique. He said stubbornness—a resolute indignation—took hold of his heart. He became more determined than ever to see God's promise come to pass. He renewed his declarations to the doctors, the nurses, and to anyone who would listen that his wife would recover completely. Many felt it was delusional for Ken not to accept the doctors' prognosis. Still, Ken persisted with his faith-filled prayers and buoyant expectation.

After almost three months Ellen awoke, healed and whole in every sense. Ken's faith was justified! He had prevailed in his effort to place the truth of God's promise above natural circumstances. Ken and Ellen resumed their lives serving God and, as a glorious bonus, numerous hospital staff accepted Christ as their savior.

Standing on God's word can be challenging. But even if modern medicine offers no hope, there is still hope in God. Just ask Ken and Ellen.

Prayer

Lord, strengthen my determination to complete my journey to wholeness. Help me to hold on to you and your word. Grant me the grace to be stubborn in a good way—a way that keeps my faith strong and resolute. Amen.

Day 25

Where's the Power?

If you are battling illness and you are a mature believer, strong in faith, with a group of spiritually developed brothers and sisters in the Lord who support you, congratulations! You are well positioned for supernatural healing.

But what if you are a new believer, surrounded by people who know little or nothing about God's miraculous power? Can you still connect with God and receive your healing?

Absolutely! Healing isn't dependent on us, but on God!

It is true that we have a role to play in both believing and cooperating with God's kingdom principles. If even that sounds confusing or unfamiliar, let's make it easier. Just ask yourself, "Where's the power?"

In every community, there are Bible-believing, spirit-filled Christians, who would love nothing more than to pray with you. These are the people with whom you want to connect. Call churches that identify themselves as spirit-filled or charismatic and ask if they offer healing prayer. Look for prayer groups, Bible studies, and home fellowships that believe in the gifts of the Spirit and healing prayer. Keep it simple by asking those you contact, "Do you believe Christ offers unconditional healing through the work of the Cross, just as He offers salvation?" If they do, Bingo! If not, thank them for their time and move on. You are looking for people who are familiar with—and operate in—the power of God. Accept nothing less!

You can also connect to God's power from other sources: anointed music, CDs, DVDs, books (I once received a tremendous healing while reading a book on healing), television, the Internet, or wherever God leads you. These are important resources you can tap into on a daily basis. You can't overdose on God! Saturate yourself with anything truly of His spirit. It isn't just the truth of God that makes us free. It is the power that is found in His manifest presence. Connect to it and you will find freedom!

Prayer

Lord, I thank you for Divine connections,

both with you and the people you desire to

minister to my life. I ask you to lead me to

resources that will facilitate your healing

power in me. Thank you, Lord. Amen.

Day 26

Faith Busters (Part 1)

In the devotions titled "Single Minded" and "Thought Life," we learned the importance of resisting thoughts contrary to God's word and will for our lives. These dark thoughts assault our faith and our belief in the goodness of God. They are lies coming from the "father of lies" (Jn 8:44), and if not forcefully addressed, will hinder or block our connection to God's power.

Over time, one expects these demonic assaults. After all, this is what Satan does. What most Christians rarely expect are faith-busting attacks, delivered by friends or ministries.

For example, have you ever heard a Christian friend, relative, or minister, make a statement similar to "the days of healing are past" or "God is getting glory from your sickness"? How about, "It may not be God's will to heal you" or "God is trying to teach or correct you through sickness"?

Talk about faith-busters! How does one receive from God when doubt-filled words, ostensibly validated by their proclamation from a pulpit or a spiritual friend, contradict the scriptural principles on which we are staking our healing—even our lives?

This is where unshakeable faith in the truth and power of God's word is required. Regardless of their origins, we need to recognize the faith-rattling statements mentioned above are un-scriptural. The Bible specifically rejects ambiguity regarding God's will to heal, instead giving repeated assurance and comfort. Added to that is the example of Jesus and His ministry on earth (including unconditional healing), signifying what He now makes available to everyone through the power of the Cross. Spiritually and emotionally, we need to seize this truth and identify with it. We need to make it our own, rejecting all destructive contradictions. Maintaining the purity of our beliefs is vital and achieved when we reject non-Biblical teachings, even when they come from seemingly qualified sources. Whenever you are in doubt, put your trust in His word—in His love for you—and in doing so, keep your faith connection strong!

Prayer

God, I trust in your love and faithfulness
to me. Please keep my faith and focus
strong. By the power of your Spirit, help
me to hear from you and your word clearly.
Thank you, Lord. Amen.

Day 27

Faith Busters (Part 2)

Because of the harmful impact that faith-busting, connection-robbing statements can have, let's examine some of them in depth.

Let's start with "The days of healing are past." If that is true, then the days of salvation are also gone since one hundred and nine times the Bible uses the same Greek word (sozo) for healing as it does for salvation. In addition, the Lord commands Christians to heal the sick as well as teach salvation, an edict as divine today as it was two thousand years ago (Mk 16:15-18).

How about "God gets glory from our sickness"? If that is true, why did Jesus heal anyone? Then consider Matthew 15:30-31, which tells us God was glorified *after* Jesus healed the sick, not before. Moreover, John 15:8 makes it clear that God is glorified by our productivity as opposed to the incapacitation caused by illness.

Another common assertion is "It may not be God's will to heal you." Now that is a harsh thought! Thank goodness it has no scriptural foundation. The Word makes it clear that God sees and treats all people as equal (Acts 10:34, Gal 2:6). If He has healed *one* person, then *everyone* is eligible. Otherwise, God is showing favoritism.

Finally, let's look at "God is trying to teach or correct you through sickness." Diametrically opposed to 2 Timothy 3:16, which emphatically declares that God teaches and corrects through His word, this statement implies that God joins with demonic workings to impact our lives. The truth is that He does the opposite, working now, as He did on earth, "…healing all who were oppressed by the devil" (Acts 10:38).

God is a perfect parent to His children. Just as good parents love, nurture, and bless their children's lives, God does so and more. He never denies us what we need (Ps 34:10) and He is faithful to us for all our lives (2 Tim 2:13). Trust in that and your faith won't be "busted." It will only grow!

Prayer

Father, you are a perfect parent to me. I believe you always have my best interest at heart. Thank you for watching over me so lovingly. I trust in you for all my needs, including healing. Amen.

Day 28

The Place To Be

Whom do you like to spend time with? Most people prefer the company of fun, enthusiastic, optimistic people. There is a reason for this, and it relates to the way God created us. Just as sunlight nurtures our natural surroundings, positive interactions enrich our soul.

When dealing with illness, consistent interaction with life-giving moments is essential. These activities can take many forms, such as walking in the woods, reading a book, or having a meal with friends. The point is, we are nourished when we interact with the people and things God created us to enjoy.

What about our interactions with God? What can we expect to come of those? For the person battling sickness, God offers only that which is good, positive, and life affirming. For those discouraged by the ravages of infirmity, He offers assurance and hope. For the weak and illness-weary, He gives strength and joy. For the scared, His love expels fear. For the hurting, He pours out comfort.

This is what God does! This is what He will do for you! When you ask Him to be the Lord of your life, you get *all* of Him—nothing held back. You get His full attention, His love, mercy, and grace. You get His best, you get all He is, and you get His heart!

Settle the truth of this in your heart. Open yourself to Him. Even if being transparent or vulnerable is something that doesn't come easily, give it a try with God. Tell Him what you are feeling and what you are concerned about. Express thanksgiving for the blessings in your life. Be honest about the things that make you anxious. Talk to Him the way you talk to your closest friend. Be real—be human!

What you experience in return may astonish you. To spend time with God is to spend time in the most glorious place this life has to offer. He is waiting for you right now. Do you have a better place to be?

Prayer

Lord, thank you for being so accessible.
Even now, I delight in speaking to you and
listening for your voice. Help me remember
I can include you in everything I do. I love
you, Lord. Amen.

Day 29

Keep Your Healing

It is important to remember that illness can be affected by both realms of the spirit—the divine and the dark. This is logical when you consider we are eternal spirit beings living in earthly physical bodies. Healing occurs when the power of God, which exists in the spirit realm, manifests in the natural realm—our bodies.

Unfortunately, this spiritual sensitivity also opens us to physical attacks from the demonic realm. This dark power is dedicated to harming anyone it can. It is the root of all things evil and works in opposition to God's desire for our lives.

Whether your healing is instant or progressive, be aware that Satan will seek to sabotage or steal it altogether. He will assault your emotions, attack your faith, and try to destroy your hope and peace. Don't be intimidated by this—it is simply what he does. Knowing his tactics enables you to render him powerless.

When it comes to dealing with this wicked harassment, follow the advice of the apostle James: "Resist the devil and he will flee from you" (Jas 4:7). By recognizing any demonic effort and resisting Satan's lies, you render him ineffective. If he brings discouragement, worship God with your favorite music. If he assaults your faith, meditate on God's faithfulness—His commitment to your life. If he tries to make you feel isolated and alone, get strengthened by the fellowship and prayer of a close friend. Above all else, call out to God. Let His spirit refresh you. Let Him comfort your heart and ignite your faith. Let Him fight on your behalf!

In Christ you have what darkness can never vanquish. You have pure love, seamlessly connected from God's heart to yours. Focus on it. Feed on it. Let it protect you and the healing God is doing in your life. Glory to God, it is all you will ever need!

Prayer

Lord, as your loved and protected child, I declare the failure of all dark efforts brought against me. By word and thought, I resist Satan and expect him to flee. I do so in the precious name of Jesus. Amen.

Day 30

More Than a Gift

It is a wonderful thing to receive a healing touch from God. There is something exhilarating and wonderful in the way it affects the soul. Though we obtain healing the same way we acquire every blessing from God (by grace through faith), experiencing divine healing can be uniquely life changing. My first encounter with God's healing power was so profound it altered the course of my life, ultimately leading to my entrance into ministry.

At the heart of this heavenly blessing lies an often missed truth. Healing isn't simply a gift from God—healing *is* God. Just as the Bible identifies God *as* love, it also reveals Him in this specific light. Stated another way, no distinction can be made between God and His blessings because by definition He *is* those things. He *is* love. He *is* peace. He *is* healing.

Why is this important? Because understanding God's nature and character allows us to relate to—and receive from—our perfect union with Him. It inspires our faith to realize we are always in contact with healing because we are always in contact with God. Every part of His being seeks to heal every part of our lives—because healing is who He is.

Meditate on this and let it permeate your spirit. If you have been plagued by doubts or anxiety regarding His willingness to heal, consider that God would have to alter His very being—His existence—to withhold healing from you. Scripture tells us this is impossible. God proclaims in Malachi 3:6 "I am the Lord, I do not change."

Please take this to heart. It is important to see God as He exists, not just for what He does. In doing so, we place our focus where it belongs, and we deepen our relationship with Him. We see healing as not just a *gift* but as a *person*. Remember, God heals—not because He can—but because it is who He is!

Prayer

Lord, I acknowledge who you are, not just what you do. You are love, you are peace, and you are healing. Through my union with you, all these things are available to me. I gratefully and lovingly receive them now. Amen.

Healing Scriptures

The Bible is filled with stories of God's healing power, which demonstrate His desire to minister healing to us. The following verses are a sample of God's promises to us—both to heal and help us with any need.

Psalm 30:2

Oh Lord my God, I cried out to You, and You healed me.

Psalm 103:2-3

Bless the Lord, Oh my soul, and forget not all His benefits:
Who forgives all your iniquities, Who heals all your diseases.

Psalm 107:20

He sent His word and healed them, and delivered them from their destructions.

Proverbs 4:20-22

My son, give attention to my words; incline your ear to my sayings.

Do not let them depart from your eyes; keep them in the midst of your heart.

For they are life to those who find them, and health to all their flesh.

Isaiah 41:10

Fear not, for I am with you; be not dismayed for I am your God. I will strengthen you, Yes, I will help you. I will uphold you with my righteous right hand.

Isaiah 53:4-5

Surely He has borne our griefs [sicknesses] and carried our sorrows [pains], yet we esteemed Him stricken, smitten by God and afflicted.

But He was wounded for our transgressions, He was bruised for your iniquities, the chastisement for our peace was upon Him, and by His stripes we are healed.

Jeremiah 17:14

Heal me, O Lord, and I shall be healed; save me and I shall be saved, for You are my praise.

Matthew 8:16-17

When evening had come, the brought to Him many who were demon-possessed. And He cast out the spirits with a word, and healed all who were sick, that it might be fulfilled which was spoken by Isaiah the prophet, saying: "He Himself took our infirmities and bore our sicknesses."

Matthew 9:35

Then Jesus went about all the cities and villages, teaching in their synagogues, preaching the gospel of the kingdom, and healing every sickness and every disease among the people.

Matthew 11:28-30

"Come to me, all you who labor and are heavy laden, and I will give you rest. Take My yoke upon you and learn from Me, for I am gentle and lowly in heart, and you will find rest for your souls. For My yoke is easy and My burden is light."

Matthew 12:15

...great multitudes followed Him, and He healed them all.

Mark 11:23-24

"For assuredly, I say to you, whoever says to this mountain, 'Be removed and be cast into the sea,' and does not doubt in his heart, but believes that those things he says will be done, he will have whatever he says.

Therefore I say to you, whatever things you ask when you pray, believe that you receive then and you will have them."

John 10:10

"The thief does not come except to steal, and to kill, and to destroy. I have come that they may have life, and that they may have it more abundantly."

John 14:13

"...whatever you ask in My name, that I will do, that the Father may be glorified in the Son."

John 15:7

"If you abide in Me, and My words abide in you, you will ask what you desire, and it shall be done for you."

Acts 5:16

Also a multitude gathered from the surrounding cities to Jerusalem, bringing sick people and those who were tormented by unclean spirits, and they were all healed.

Acts 10:38

"...God anointed Jesus of Nazareth with the Holy Spirit and with power, who went about doing good and healing all who were oppressed by the devil, for God was with Him."

Romans 8:32

He who did not spare His own Son, but delivered Him up for us all, how shall He not with Him also freely give us all things?

Hebrews 4:16

Let us therefore come boldly to the throne of grace, that we may obtain mercy and find grace to help in time of need.

Hebrews 10:23

Let us hold fast the confession of our hope without wavering, for He who promised is faithful.

James 1:17

Every good gift and every perfect gift is from above, and comes down from the Father of lights, with whom there is no variation or shadow of turning.

1 Peter 2:24

Who Himself bore our sins in His own body on the tree [Cross], that we, having died to sins, might live for righteousness—by whose stripes you were healed.

3 John 2

Beloved, I pray that you may prosper in all things and be in health, just as your soul prospers.

Contact

Paul prays this devotional has blessed your life. You can contact him regarding this book, or any other ministry matter at PaulRichardsMinistries.org. You may write him at:

Paul Richards Ministries
PO Box 3088
Durango, CO 81302

Acknowledgements

Few accomplishments in life
are obtained without assistance.
My gratitude to those who, with this project,
confirmed this truth.

Lynn Kuntz

Weston Bennett

Lauren Brombert

Suzanne Parrott

98794904R00046

Made in the USA
Columbia, SC
06 July 2018